Walking in the City with
JANE

To my lovely cousin Nancy Hughes; her husband, Ian; and their son, Alexander Boyce — S.H.
À ma sœur Isabelle — V.B.

Text © 2018 Susan Hughes
Illustrations © 2018 Valérie Boivin

Kids Can Press gratefully acknowledges the financial support of the Government of Ontario, through the Ontario Media Development Corporation; the Ontario Arts Council; the Canada Council for the Arts; and the Government of Canada, through the CBF, for our publishing activity.

Published in Canada and the U.S. by Kids Can Press Ltd.
25 Dockside Drive, Toronto, ON M5A 0B5

Kids Can Press is a Corus Entertainment Inc. company

www.kidscanpress.com

The artwork in this book was rendered in Photoshop.
The text is set in Rotis Sans Serif.

Photo credit, page 36: Jane Jacobs outside her home on Spadina Avenue in Toronto, December 21, 1968 (Frank Lennon /*Toronto Star*/Getty Images)

Edited by Stacey Roderick and Katie Scott
Designed by Marie Bartholomew

Printed and bound in Malaysia, in 9/2017 by Tien Wah Press (Pte) Ltd

CM 18 0 9 8 7 6 5 4 3 2 1

Library and Archives Canada Cataloguing in Publication

Hughes, Susan, 1960 –, author
Walking in the city with Jane: a story of Jane Jacobs / written by Susan Hughes; illustrated by Valérie Boivin.

ISBN 978-1-77138-653-1 (hardcover)

I. Boivin, Valérie 1980 –, illustrator II. Title.

PS8565.U42W35 2018   jC813'.54   C2017-903221-6

Walking in the City with
JANE

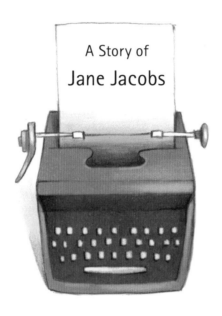

A Story of
Jane Jacobs

Written by **Susan Hughes**

Illustrated by **Valérie Boivin**

Kids Can Press

Jane sighed. *When will the lunch bell ring?* she wondered.

It was uncomfortable holding her book under her desk and sneaking peeks when Miss Kortright wasn't looking. Jane wished she could be out on her bike instead. Or learning something interesting.

Nothing was worse than being bored.

Suddenly, Jane's eyes opened wide. Now *this* was interesting.

Miss Kortright was demonstrating something called a toothbrush. Jane had never seen one of these before! None of the children had.

"You all must promise to brush your teeth every day for the rest of your lives," her teacher ordered.

Jane knew a promise was a serious thing. She also knew she couldn't be certain that she'd brush her teeth *every single day for the rest of her life*! So Jane refused to promise. Not only that, she encouraged her classmates to do the same.

An angry Miss Kortright sent her home.

But Jane didn't really mind. She learned the most when she was out and about. She enjoyed looking closely at things she saw around her. Sometimes she tested herself by explaining things to her imaginary friends Benjamin Franklin, Thomas Jefferson and Cerdic.

"How does that work?" Cerdic might ask, pointing to a car or a traffic light. "What is it for?" He was from medieval times, so Jane had to explain almost *everything* to him.

After finishing high school, Jane went to live with her older sister, Betty, in New York City. Her sister worked there as a salesgirl in a department store.

Jane loved her hometown, but *this* city was huge and exciting. Day after day, Jane looked for work, but she also enjoyed getting off the subway at different stops and exploring whatever neighborhood she found.

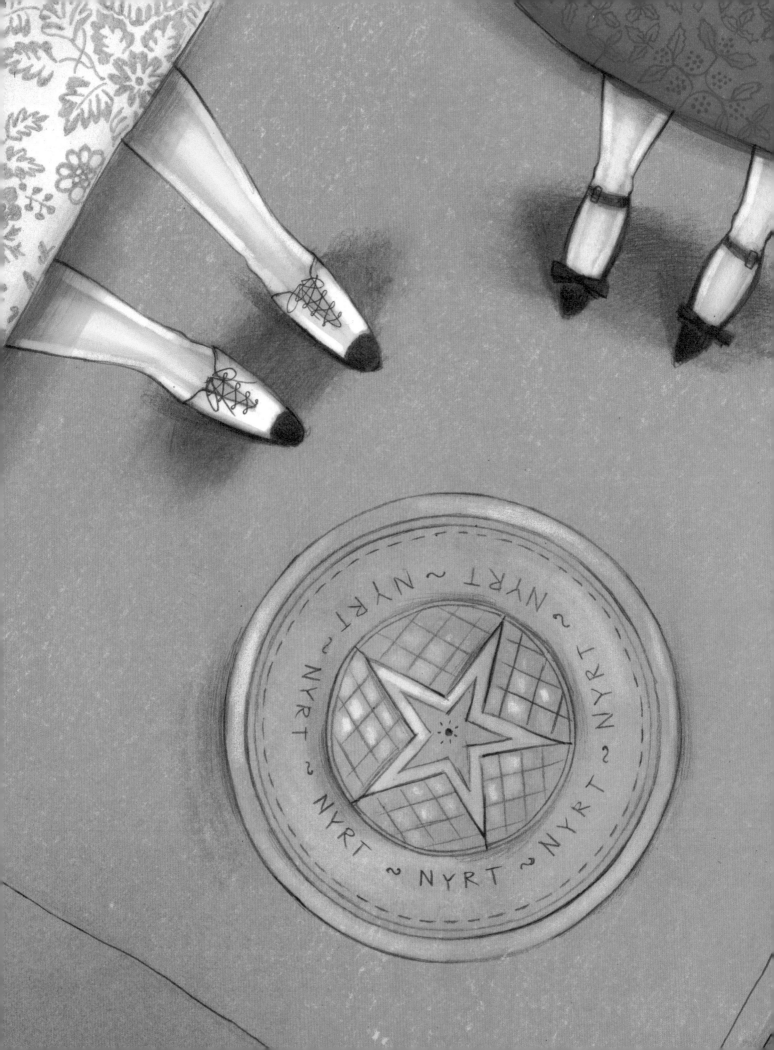

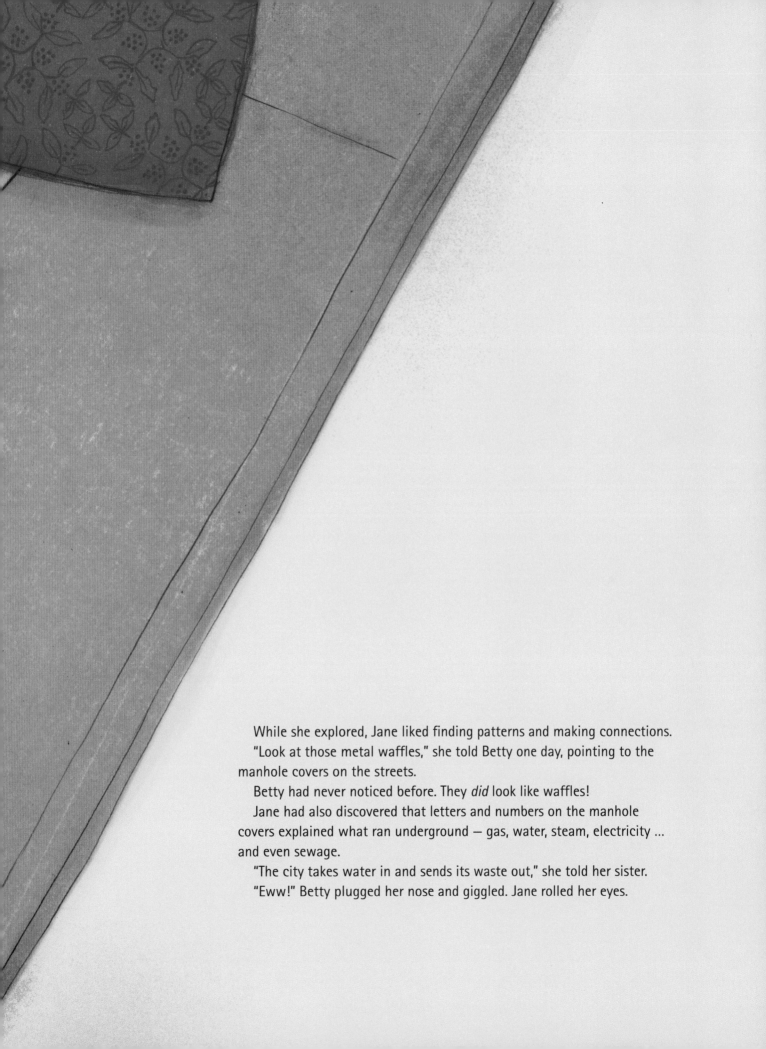

While she explored, Jane liked finding patterns and making connections.

"Look at those metal waffles," she told Betty one day, pointing to the manhole covers on the streets.

Betty had never noticed before. They *did* look like waffles!

Jane had also discovered that letters and numbers on the manhole covers explained what ran underground — gas, water, steam, electricity ... and even sewage.

"The city takes water in and sends its waste out," she told her sister.

"Eww!" Betty plugged her nose and giggled. Jane rolled her eyes.

On another day, Jane discovered something else about how cities worked. She knew that animals, plants, rivers, sunshine and rain all worked together as part of a healthy ecosystem. "But a city is *also* an ecosystem," she realized. "It is made of different parts — sidewalks, parks, stores, neighborhoods, City Hall ... and people, of course. When they all work together, the city is healthy."

Now *this* was interesting!

"Large cities that work well might look messy, but they're really not," Jane told her friend Bob Jacobs. He was an architect. They were walking along a street, looking for a good place to eat.

"Healthy cities need a mix of buildings that are used for different activities and filled with different types of people," explained Jane. "Healthy cities are places where people can live and work safely and happily."

"I see," said Bob, staring at Jane.

"And look!" Jane stopped in front of a perfect little restaurant, one she had never seen before. "Short city blocks give people more opportunities to turn corners, more chances to meet up with others, more possibilities for surprises like this one! And that makes people happy, too!"

"It would make *me* happy if you would marry me," said Bob.

After Jane and Bob were married, Jane continued to work as a journalist. She and Bob were also busy raising their three children: Jimmy, Ned and Burgin.

The Jacobs family lived above a candy shop. They loved the activity that swirled around their lively neighborhood.

"All these people out and about!" Jane would say to her children. "All in the same space and all doing different things — chatting, shopping, working, relaxing ... It's like a sidewalk ballet, isn't it?"

Jane thought of cities as places for communities of people. However, many experts thought cities were mainly for big businesses and that new was always better than old.

These city planners labeled several older neighborhoods in New York "slums" that were unfit for people to live in. They decided to bulldoze them and build block after block of identical high-rise buildings in their place.

Upset, Jane wrote an article criticizing the plan. She had visited new developments like these in other cities. They had looked so empty and unfriendly.

And then one day, Jane learned that a powerful city planner named Robert Moses had labeled *her* neighborhood a slum. He wanted to tear down part of it to build a highway. The four lanes of highway would also replace a small road through the local park.

Why? So traffic could get downtown more easily.

Jane couldn't stand by and let this happen. She and her family joined their neighbors at rallies and in writing letters of protest.

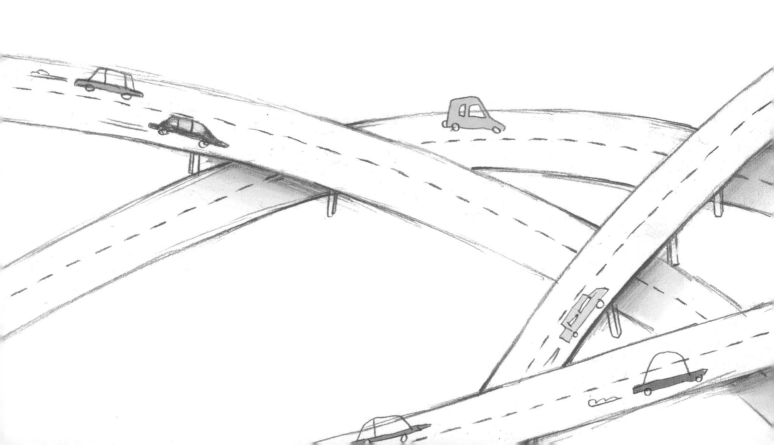

On the day that Robert Moses spoke about his plans at a city meeting, he glared at Jane and the other protestors.

"There is nobody against this," he complained to the city officials, "NOBODY, NOBODY, NOBODY but a bunch of ... a bunch of MOTHERS!"

Robert Moses didn't seem to care what the community thought.

Jane and the others refused to give up. They even convinced the city to temporarily close the park to traffic. This gave Jane an idea. People had ribbon-*cutting* ceremonies to celebrate the *opening* of new places. Why not celebrate *closing* the park to traffic with a special ribbon-*tying* ceremony?

So they did. Jane's three-year-old daughter, Burgin, and a friend tied a ribbon across the marble arch at the park entrance. "The park is closed to traffic!" they cheered.

Eventually, the city officials agreed to cancel the plan for the highway *and* keep the park closed to traffic for good.

But according to Robert Moses, cities were created by and for traffic. Two years later, he came up with another plan for a highway — eight lanes running right through the center of the city!

Believing cities were created by and for *people*, Jane led a fight against the highway. After several months, the community protests won out and the expressway was canceled!

Another two years went by, and the expressway was proposed *again*. This time, it got the go-ahead.

Once more Jane sprang into action. She organized rallies and protests. One day, she and several other activists interrupted a city meeting about the plan. The police were called, and Jane was arrested.

Jane was soon freed, but by then she was a local hero, and her arrest
had caused a big stir. New Yorkers were outraged that officials would
go to such extremes to defend their plan. This became a turning point,
and the city canceled the expressway.

Jane and the other "nobodies" had made a difference once again.

A few months later, Jane and her family moved to Toronto, Canada — another big city.

She soon felt right at home, exploring the streets of her new city. And almost immediately, she found herself speaking out — this time against an expressway designed to cut through her new neighborhood. Once again, Jane's voice helped win the day, and the construction was halted.

Throughout her lifetime and beyond, Jane Jacobs urged
city planners to make cities better for the people living in
them. She inspired communities to take a stand for their
neighborhoods. She also encouraged everyone living in cities
to look around them while they walked and to listen, linger
and think about what they saw.

After all, they just might discover something interesting!

Author's Note

Walking in the City with Jane is a fictionalized account of the life of the influential writer and urban thinker Jane Jacobs. The story and illustrations in the book are based on actual events and photographs.

Jane was born in Scranton, Pennsylvania, in 1916 and moved to New York City in 1934. Years later, in 1968, she and her family moved to Toronto, Canada. Although Jane did not receive a college degree, she took many college courses on topics that interested her. All her life she asked questions, made observations and shared her ideas. She worked as a journalist and wrote many books, including the world-famous *The Death and Life of Great American Cities*. In it, she explained her views about cities being urban ecosystems, what made them work — and what could make them great.

Today, people — both children and adults — continue to follow her example of adventuring out into the city streets. To look up at the power lines and peer down at the manhole covers. To sit on park benches and pop into train stations. To appreciate and be part of a "sidewalk ballet." To learn about their cities firsthand, the way she did. Jane Jacobs became a Canadian citizen in 1974. She died in 2006, at age 89.

Celebrating Jane Jacobs

To honor Jane, some of her friends and colleagues started a series of free walks led by local citizens who share facts and stories about their communities and help bring them to life for others. Now held in many cities across the world, the tours inspire people to connect with their neighbors and their cities. You can find out more by visiting www.janeswalk.org or www.janejacobswalk.org.